The Kenneth Smith Story
Through Blood, Tears and Sweat
By Kenneth Smith

The Kenneth Smith Story

© 2018 by Kenneth Smith

ISBN # 978-1-387-65279-2

All rights reserved. No part of this book may be reproduced in any form without permission in writing from author. Reviewers may quote brief passages in reviews.

Disclaimer

No part of this book may be reproduced or transmitted in any form by any means, mechanical or electronic, including photocopying or recording, or by any information storage and retrieval system, or transmitted by email without permission in writing from the publisher.

Table of Contents

Dedication	4
Introduction	5
Chapter 1: How It All Began	6
Chapter 2: School Days	8
Chapter 3: When I Met God	14
Chapter 4: Dropped Off In Hell	16
Chapter 5: Fighting Through It	18
Chapter 6: God's Plan for You	20
Chapter 7: Trapped Inside of "No"	22
Chapter 8: Becoming A Man	24
Chapter 9: He Protected Me	25
Chapter 10: When the Tears Dry Up	27
Contact Info.	29
Notes	30

Dedication

This book is dedicated to every person in my life that saw a story in me and told me I could do it. Also to my uncle Jerry R.I.P, my grandfather and grandmother R.I.P. To my mother, a real hero in my eyes for showing me that anything is possible through prayer. To Minister Laretha Johnson, my Auntie who first inspired me to pick up a pencil to write my problems away. To my brothers and sister for fighting the fight with me. To my kids for giving me a reason to wake up. To God for trusting me with another chance to fulfill His plan for my life!

Introduction

My prayer is that you will be blessed by this book and that your life will be changed. That you will look at your trials through a different eye. That you will see Jesus in every trial in your life and trust God in your weakest moments.

MAY GOD BLESS YOU!

Chapter 1

How It All Began

I am writing this book hoping that it will change the way we treat kids and that serves as a testimony of forgiveness. I was born on September 24, 1977 to Harold A. Sawyer and Bernice A. Smith. My father grew up in a broken home and my mother had both parents in the home. I really don't remember a lot about my dad.

One of my most vivid memories is of my dad racing with my brother and me. We would run and run, trying to win the race, but my dad was so fast, we could never win! However, we had so much fun just being together and laughing!

When my dad wasn't racing with me and my brother, he was beating on my mother. Sometimes I loved my dad and other times I hated him for how he abused my mother. He would lock me and my brother in a closet when he'd jump on my mom. We would hear our mom hollering and crying for help. We never knew what to expect from our father. At the time, I didn't know my dad was using drugs and drinking alcohol heavily.

A father is a very important factor in the home. He is the one who sets the tone and foundation for the home, and when there is no father in the home, the home is left open for all kinds of attacks to happen naturally, physically and spiritually.

Some men want their kids to be great but without their presence and support. They show up at football games yelling, "That's my boy!" but never throw a ball with him, and get upset when that son quits things in life. Kids only know what we teach them through the life we live.

I was only four years old when my dad started beating on my mom but I can remember it like it was yesterday. At the time we lived with a man; He was nice but he was scared of my dad so he never tried to stop my dad from beating on my mom. We weren't supposed to even be living with him. We would have to hide when the rent man came to the house.

One of the most important things about being a father and the head of the house is to be a provider, and to provide a home to be the head of. My mother had three kids at the time: me, my older brother and my younger brother. My younger brother lived with my auntie and would come over to the house to visit with us.

We lived the majority of our childhood in poverty, being homeless, displaced and exposed to physical, mental and substance abuse.

Chapter 2

School Days

It was really hard in school, having to go not knowing where you would sleep when you got out of school. I learned about faith before I ever knew anything about church. I had to have faith that my mom would be there to get me when I got out of school, and if she was; where would we spend the night? I didn't ask where we were going to stay; there is a great difference between spending the night somewhere and staying somewhere. Spending the night somewhere you are in a temporary place for that night, and then having to leave for whatever reason. To stay somewhere means you plan to live at this place and call it home.

One day I was at school about to dress out for gym. My shoes had a hole at the bottom of them and smelled badly. When I noticed one of my classmates had left his shoes in the gym, I took them and put them on, as if they were mine. When the young man saw I had his shoes on, he became angry, making fun of how poor I was. The only friends I had were poor friends like me. I understand now that it is easy to be around people that live like you. I would try to hang around kids in school that I thought were cool, hoping I would be more like them. Sometimes I would wake up hoping that I would have a different life. I was so tired of being poor, that I would cry from realizing my life was still the same.

There were times we would walk around with a bag of clothes all day, and that would be the only clothing we had. Many times, my brother and I were slapped and beaten for not wanting to walk anymore. It was hard having to walk everywhere we went. We never owned a car, so on cold and a lot of hot days, I would sit down on the sidewalk and refuse to go any further until I got something to drink. I can remember crying and feeling like I was about to pass out. As a child, I remember just wishing I had a cup of water to drink, or a sandwich to eat. It seemed as if we were never going to stop walking. We would see people we knew pass us by all the time, but no one would stop.

During that time, some days the only thing we would have to eat was what we called flour bread, which is flour and water mix together and fried. Some days it would be just grits and butter.

A lot of kids don't know how blessed they are to have two parents in the house that love them more than they love themselves. It is so important that we help our kids to understand that there are some kids that don't have what they have, in hopes of them behaving better and knowing they could be worse off than they are.

Children don't ask to be here, only God can give life. God trusts us to be good parents. It is important to make sure we bring them up in the ways of God's word. Children only know what we show them, and look up to us as a role model, so you should never tell your child to "do as you say and not as you do." Too many times we kill our kid's dreams by being a bad influence; often times before they ever know how to dream. It was a dream of mine to just take a hot bath, to wash the dirt off my feet, or to wear clean clothes. I would dream that I had parents that loved me more than the drugs they were using. It was hard trying live as a child, but being forced to be a man. I found myself at times, being disrespectful to adults. The first thing my family would say is "wait a minute, you are not grown." I would respond by saying: *I take care of myself, what do you call that?*

Your child is a seed, and you are in charge of it. Just as a plant needs sunlight, your child needs love. Just as a plant needs water, your child needs direction!

I wanted to give up many times when I was homeless down in Jacksonville, FL., but the only thing that gave me hope was knowing I was different and I could see victory. I just didn't know how long I would have to wait to get it. I need you to understand that my parents never had a house of their own. We would walk from house to house looking for a place to spend the night. A lot of the houses we stayed at were drug houses. We stayed at some family homes; some no better than others because of the way we were treated.

I can remember my mother, my brother and I sleeping on the front porch of some family member's house many nights while they were inside in their warm beds. We have even slept in cars outside of people's houses. It is so important that we treat people like we want to be treated. It doesn't matter if you are a man/woman, boy or girl if you are hurting, then, I am hurting. If you are without clothes then I'll clothe you. I know my mom and dad would have loved me. I never got to meet my real dad before he died. I got to know Harold Sawyer, the drunken drug addict. I often wondered what my real father was like.

I would meet different men that my mom would take me around. If they were nice, with a nice house and car, I would tell my mom to marry him because we were tired of walking and having nowhere to live. My mother, like many others on drugs, really only wanted to be with men that were on drugs which I could not understand at all. The first step to being drug free is to change the friends that can stop you from being successful. We also need to be careful who we bring around our kids. So many times we think our kids will forget about what they have seen us do. Sometimes your kids remember what you forget.

I remember my mother taking me and my brothers to the PIC N' Save store where we would meet my god daddy. My god daddy was a white man named Charles English. My mother says she met him when she was about twenty-one years old. She said after sleeping with him only once, they remained friends. He began giving her $25.00 every other day and he would even give more money over the last 16 years when we needed it. My brothers and I never got new clothes for school, summer nor winter. The only clothes we ever had were year round. Thanks God for my god daddy, he would take us to the second hand store sometimes to get clothes and shoes.

Going to the second hand store for us, was a blessing. Even though it was not brand new clothes, it was more than we had. It was hard to keep up with the clothes that he would buy us; from not being able to wash them, to sleeping in different places every night, or just plain losing them from place to place. I can remember Charles met my mother, my brothers and I downtown to give us some money. A police officer saw my brother and I going to his car. We were only about six and seven. The officer asked if we were ok, and before we could answer, my god daddy said to the officer, "They are ok. I would never hurt them." I knew from that day on that he really cared about us.

The relationship my mom and god father had was so different that I would watch to see if she was doing anything with him for this money, but I never saw anything that made me think she was. She would send us to him to get the money every other day so sometimes they never saw each other at all. It took me a long time to really understand that their relationship was not at all about sex, which is all I ever saw men wanting from my mom. My god dad showed me how to help people without cost, or looking for something in return. He showed me how to love people that don't look like you or act like you, and to never limit your blessings by looking for them to come from one direction.

For Christmas my god dad would buy us bikes and toys, but when we would go to sleep my mom and step dad would sell them for drugs. We never got a chance to enjoy any holidays, they were like any other day to us. It was hard looking at other kids playing with their toys they got for Christmas when we didn't have any.

Some people can speak good things about you and your life; they can even see you having a house one day. But be careful, some people like it when you are down so we have to watch who we hang around. I had no one to show my report card to. My mom never really acted as if she cared about my grades. My dad left my mom with all of the responsibility of raising us. When my brother and I reached the age nine and up, we started living with relatives. It is good to have family but sometimes family is not good for each other. If you do something for someone, you should never talk about it even if you are mad at the person you helped. Because of family, I had to overcome family hurt. Sometimes family will hurt you worse than a friend. In the eyesight of God we all are family and God has assigned us to be responsible for each other. Because I did not have the help I needed from my family, I began to skip school in the sixth grade. I was not a bad kid but I ran with bad people, so I looked bad.

Chapter 3

When I Met God

While in middle school, I started going to church every now and then. The first church I went to was a large church in downtown Jacksonville, FL. They gave us clothes and food. One day the preacher asked me if I wanted to be baptized, and I said yes. That was my first meaningful experience with church. All my prior visits to were because of a girl, and I really didn't like the teaching aspect of church. I wasn't open to receive the full essence of church and fellowship because I felt church people were mean and weren't genuine.

Later, I began visiting my uncle and aunt's church; it was there on a Sunday morning as I walked into service that I was slayed on the floor by the spirit of God and God spoke to me for the first time. God showed me that He already knew everything that was happening in my life. His spirit comforted me and assured me that He would never leave me nor forsake me and would always be with me.

At the age of eleven years old, He gave me a revelation of many things to come. My brother And I would walk from home to church because we were dealing with so much pressure from every side. We pressed our way through day by day. On the way to church, God would deal with us, we would open up to each other and talk about things that we knew we couldn't change. On the inside we trusted that God would change these things. It is hard to have faith in things you can't see.

My brother and I loved going to church and singing. Sometimes, I believe that was his way of escaping. I liked going to church for the cookies but mostly for my pastor. The more we went to church, the more things started to become harder for us. My brother and I would walk several miles just to get to church.

I was learning to pray. I remember my first prayer was for my mother, but by this time my mother was starting to really give up on me. I think my mother really did love my brother and me, but at that time, she loved drugs more. By this time, I started praying and asking God to kill me or forgive me when I killed myself. I felt like I couldn't endure the hurt, pain and emptiness any longer.

Chapter 4

Dropped Off In Hell

At the age of thirteen, I was released to myself and was told in so many words *catch you when I catch you* by some of my family: at that time in my life I thought I had been dropped off in hell with no way out! I can remember going to family member's houses for a place to spend the night and they said, "I can't help you, try to find your momma." I tried to tell them that my momma couldn't be found. At that time I realized that I was really on my own. I also thought that I was in my worst state, looking for rest and completion. I know God was with me as I would walk through bad areas. Life told me I needed to kill myself, and there was no reason for me to live.

At this time, my mom and I would barely see each other at all. I would stay where I could. I found myself sleeping in a place I never would have imagined I'd stay. I must admit the place was very big and cold and hot depending on the weather. This place of rest and refuge was at a park in the dug-out on a baseball field. It's amazing how one day you really hate being somewhere or doing something but over time that place or thing becomes your best friend! I started living the life I knew God had for me inside my mind which would help me to be in a totally different place than I was physically. The bible states that *we should reach a place in God where our mind becomes renewed.*

Many good people are in jail, on drugs or dead in the natural and (or) spiritual because they never let God renew their mind. God is knocking at the door of your life; will you or have you already let Him in? I spent many cold nights sleeping on the streets, with no food, walking 10-25 miles for a dollar to get food, cookies and a small fruit juice to drink.... God has been good to me!

Chapter 5

Fighting Through It

I never thought I would face a time in my life where I didn't know if I was going to live or die. There was warfare going through my mind! My flesh would tell me it was over but the spiritual connection I had with God told me I could make it; you are more than a conqueror through Christ Jesus!

We spend so much of our time looking for things that can't be found in earthly places. They say *a mind is a terrible thing to waste* but you've already wasted it if you don't know how to use it. Sometimes I have to remind myself where I came from. This works sometimes and sometimes it doesn't.

When you come to Christ, often times, things don't get better immediately. It's a process that may take weeks, months, or even years before you see a major change in your circumstances. The biggest change you will see at first will be your final destination place. Our way of thinking has to change; if we don't change then we will find ourselves repeating the same behaviors and never understand why we are doing it nor how to stop live victoriously. The Word of God says our mind isn't His mind nor are our thought His thoughts. In the bible, the Apostle Paul spoke about us having to think ourselves happy sometimes.

My problem was not that I didn't think that God would ever answer my prayers but more so the timing of when He'd answer my prayers. Until you have become mature in your having to wait on things from God can hurt. We have to know that God will not let us down. He is a friend that sticks closer than a brother. We also have to remember that He is the same all the time. His word does not lie or return to Him void.

It is the trick of satan when we start thinking things are too hard for us to keep going or that we can't make it when we are going through trying times. God has done too much for us to give up. He is looking for people who are ready to fight a good fight for Him! We can't be in today and out tomorrow. Life is too short to play with God! Take a moment and think about what God has done for you, things you know it was God that did it and you can't give credit to anyone but God.... This is the way God planned things for our lives. It is important that we let His will be done in our lives.

Chapter 6

God's Plan for You

Often times we spend our entire childhood trying to plan our life instead of allowing God to control our life; He is the head and we are the tail of life. You will grow to learn that there's nothing too hard for God. When you were going through your last trial, you may have promised God that you will change your ways but somehow along the way, you became sidetracked and fail to the tricks of the world, and the lies of the enemy. The Lord Jesus Christ tells us to trust and lean on him, who is the author and finisher of our faith, and to put no trust in man because he will let you down every time.

Through all I have seen and been through, I've learned how to call on the name of Jesus and to trust in His name through all trials and tribulations. You have to stand firm on The Word of God, even though rain comes and the wind blows, you can't be moved. You have to be still in God or you will forever move from here to there and never reach God's divine plan for your life.

You may wonder how I am still standing when my life has been one big storm throughout the years or how I keep moving all over and everywhere. The Lord God says if we keep our mind on Him, He will keep our minds in perfect peace. It is important not to move with the wind because you can land anywhere and every time you get up you have to be rooted somewhere sooner or later. We have to be sure we are attuned in the natural and spiritual when we are seeking direction. Many times throughout my life I thought I heard God and I was far off, and it cost me many things in my life.

I have wondered many times why my life had to be the way it was. I wondered why I was poor and living in a park and for so long. I am learning that without being there I might not be where I am today. Sometimes I think I should be further in life than I am. I trust and believe God has everything all in His control and He will not put any more on me than I can bear. God has been very good to me, better than I could have ever been to myself and when you think about it, God has been better to you than you have been to yourself.

I have seen people die right before my eyes; it could have been me that He called home. God has favored some us in this life because of the things that we have been through. He has blessed some us with things that money can't buy.

Around the end of my eighth grade year, I turned sixteen. One of my friends told me the police couldn't make me go to school anymore. That was my last year in school. At that time, it seemed like dropping out of school made my life easy. I didn't have to worry about school anymore. Everything that is easy isn't always the best thing for you.

It is so easy to run from things that you don't believe you can overcome. Anyone with legs can run but a man faces problems head on even in the midst of fear and uncertainty. I had become like the people around me, running when things didn't work out my way. Trying to do what seems is just prolongs the trial for later.

Chapter 7

Trapped Inside of "No"

Living in a world where yes is a stranger, and hope is so far away but rejection was my next door neighbor. It's like trying to make something out of nothing all the time. If you believe what no tells you long enough, you will stop trying to become anything or working towards anything greater than your present state. When you are trying to reach goals, no or rejection come to make you stronger and work harder to take what the devil meant for your bad and God will make it work for your good.

I have tried to jump over no and go around no and sometimes it has worked but I always come out on top going head up with no. We run from too many things in life because we aren't expecting that answer or thing to manifest in our favor. I have found that you will face that same thing down the road, so stand like a man or woman and face it head on.

I was trapped in somewhere that felt like home because that's all I knew. How do you get out of a place mentally or spiritually when you don't even realize you are trapped? When you have been called a looser all of your life it's hard to be a winner living with a looser mindset. You must pack your bags and move to a winner's mindset. After a while you will start looking at things differently.

Living in your mind is a powerful thing because you have the power to make yourself happy and no one can stop anything you're trying to do or become. At that point you are bigger than anything or person that tries to stop you.

Sometimes people make kids suffer because they aren't happy with their parent's life choices. It doesn't make a child feel good when they come to you for help and they have to hear the negative and judgmental things you've really been wanting to voice to their parents.

We have to learn how to love people where they are at. A lot of people will never make it where you are or take the path you took. God put all kinds of people on earth for a reason/ not that all people would be the same or learn the same. When you meet people where they are at, then you are loving like Jesus loves!

Chapter 8

Becoming a Man

At the age of sixteen, I was back and forth between staying with family members and in the baseball dugout. School was no longer important to me because I didn't understand the work anymore because I was behind from missing so many days. I would skip school a lot because I couldn't take a bath and didn't want to go school dirty. By this time, I was in the eighth grade, and I was sure I had failed and was ready to drop out.

When you have been down so low and you are still standing, the devil comes at you even harder because he understands that trials like your lights being turned off isn't going to work on your anymore.

We don't get to choose our parents and our parents don't choose us. We get and they get what God gives us according to His plan for our lives. With that being said, if we know God, we have to know He had a plan for us even before we came out of the womb.

When I started living in the dugout at the baseball field, I would go to church on Sunday and Wednesdays because a lady would give me a dollar each time I went. I would leave church and go to the corner store and get a pack of cookies; these cookies had two rolls in them, I would eat a role a day along with fruit off a nearby fruit tree and drink water out of the park's fountain. This part of my life was the beginning of me becoming a man.

Chapter 9

He Protected Me

I have always been told that The Lord looks after babies and fools. I don't really know which one I was. As I walked the streets at night, The Lord was a fence all around me. Some of my most scary moments were walking the streets late at night with nowhere to go.

I would walk until I'd find a park to sleep in. I'd talk to God a lot because there was no one else to talk to. It's amazing how at your weakest moments in life, God will send His angels to protect you even on the devil's grounds. There were times I wanted to kill myself, but God is so good, His spirit travailed and made me obey His will.

Many times, I could feel the enemy trying to push me out in front of cars, but even when I wanted to do it, my legs and feet would not obey me, to God be the glory! The Lord protects us when we have a purpose in His Kingdom. He knew from the time we were in our mother's womb that He would have to fight for us daily. So He has already spoken victory over us before the battle began.

The reason we get tired on our end is because it's not our fight. We are not equipped to fight life's battles on our own. Why do we think God needs our help to fight battles, he made us, we didn't make Him. He is a protector. That's how the Lord feels when we try to take things into our own hands.

Many times, I began to get angry with The Lord because my status was the same way day after day and I got besides myself and started cursing the day I was born like Job. After God allowed me to be hungry for two days, he began to minister to me about how powerful He is and how He is in control of the food even down to birds eating. He told me for every night that I slept in that park, He dispatched an army of angels to watch over me. HE IS A PROTECTOR!

Chapter 10

When the Tears Dry Up

Many times, we face things in life that we don't understand. People in the world can be so mean and hateful sometimes. We spend so much time and energy trying to figure out what we did wrong to them. You may not have done anything to a person. Sometimes people mistreat you for no reason and you can sense it. It makes you feel uncomfortable around them because you never know what to expect from them.

People that are still hurting from past hurt often hurt people around them without realizing it. I had family that would call me bad names and it seemed to make them feel good. I now realize that they weren't happy with themselves and to make themselves feel better, they'd put other people down, even family.

You will never see the real power of God without going through a fiery trial; Power is in a trial. So many times we cry during trials but there are a lot of lessons that are learned during the midst of our trials. At sixteen years old, I started to really think about my life and what I wanted out of life.

I knew I didn't want to be a drug-dealer, a thug, a drug-addict or in jail all the time. The crazy part is, I did know what I was capable of doing or being after being told for so long that I would grow up to be nothing. Sometimes I wondered if that was true.

One day God made a promise to me that if I would trust Him, He wouldn't leave me nor forsake me. He told me to stop crying, hold my head up, and listen to His plan for my life. I dried my tears up and God started speaking to me about His plans for my life. *No more will you eat from the world's table*; He *said from now on your cup will run over and I will make your name great to the nations for my name's sake; you will preach my word to the nations in season and out of season.*

Do you know why you are or do you believe what you have been called?

I spent a lot of time crying about who I was, where I came from and about how bad my life was. Not realizing at the time how much God was protecting me from the hands of the devil, and how He would watch over me as I slept outside. My tears dried up when my mother came to God, laid the drugs down and started spending time with her grandchildren. Now, she gives them everything that the devil stole from her kids. The mother I know now was the mother God had planned for me from the beginning.

To God be the glory for what He has done!

Contact Info:

Kenneth Smith

(912)242-2123

Email: Ksmith0978@live.com

Notes

Notes

Notes

Made in the USA
Coppell, TX
30 May 2022